To Joy, Joel and Honour
- fearfully and wonderfully made;
always succeed by being your amazing selves.

SaM : Brag File - A Student Progress Record

Copyright 2021, Esther Pearson

SUCCEEDING as ME

curriculum

I am

Name: _____

Contents

SUCCEEDING as ME
curriculum

Structure and Break- down

H.O.P.E.	Healthy Leadership
Self-Regulation	Problem-solving
Confidence	Connection
Self-Awareness	Empathy

ME   **WE**

Emotional Literacy

EMOTIONAL LITERACY

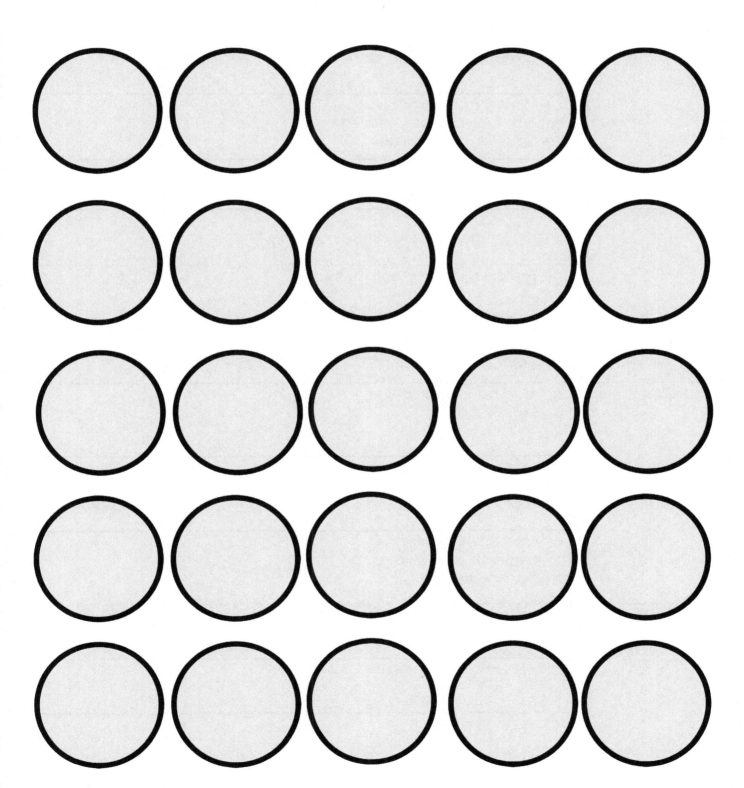

EMOTIONAL LITERACY   I can...

IDENTIFY	I can identify basic emotions such as happiness, sadness, anger and shock.	
	I can identify more subtle emotions, such as worry, contentment, irritation and boredom.	
	I can identify emotions in the times I am feeling them.	
EXPRESS	I can express a variety of emotions in safe-space drama and workshops.	
	I can express my own emotions that I feel comfortable with.	
	I can express my own emotions, even when I find them uncomfortable.	
READ	I can read basic emotions in images of others.	
	I can read basic emotions in others in safe-space drama and workshops.	
	I can read a wide variety of emotions in others in safe-space drama and workshops.	
CELEBRATION	Enjoying self – gifts, talents and abilities.	
	Achievements and victories	
	Progress and potential	

I am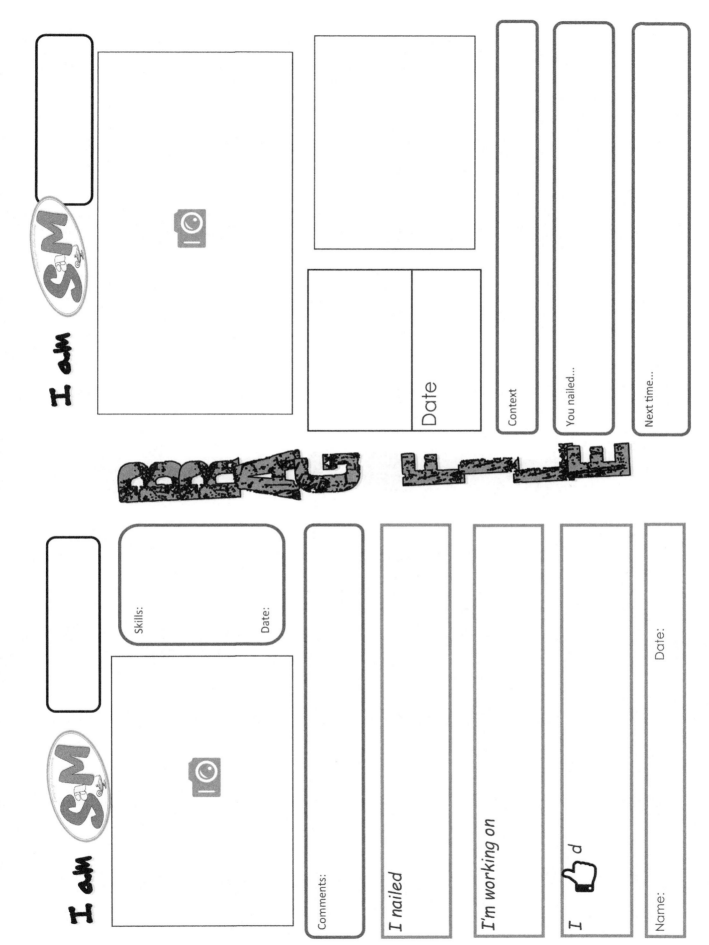

Date

Context

You nailed...

Next time...

I am

Skills:

Date:

Comments:

I nailed

I'm working on

I

Name:

Date:

7

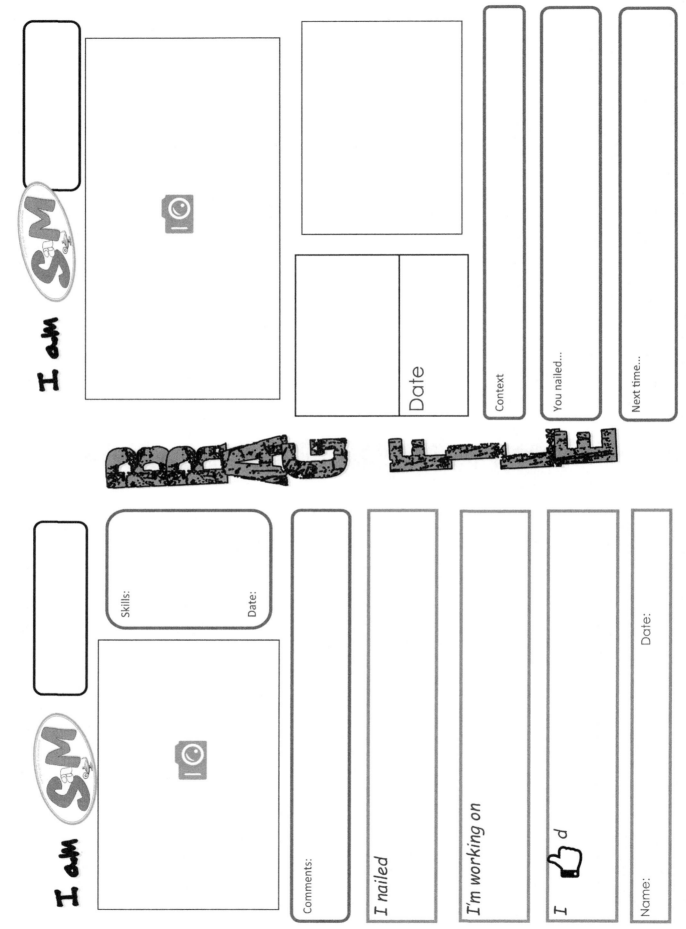

I am SM

Date

Context

You nailed...

Next time...

I am SM

Skills:

Date:

Comments:

I nailed

I'm working on

I

Name:

Date:

8

ME

Self-Awareness

Confidence
Self-Regulation
H.O.P.E.

I am

ME

SELF-AWARENESS skills overview

			Stage	
BODY	Movement	I can be still and move my body at will.		
	Control	I can use speed, touch and space appropriately.		
	Expression	I can communicate emotion with movement.		
EMOTIONS	Accurately identify feelings	I can identify 4 basic emotions.		
	Comfortable vs uncomfortable feelings	I can identify uncomfortable emotions' sensations.		
	Share personal feelings	I can share uncomfortable feelings with others.		
PERSONALITY	Personality types	I can identify basic personality types.		
	Likes and dislikes	I can identify things, actions and situations I don't like.		
	Strengths and goals	I can identify a talent, skill, strength or ability I have.		
EXPERIENCE	Core memories	I can identify a core memory.		
	Influences	I can identify an influence in my life.		
	Experience re-perceived	I can explore my actions/choices out of role.		
CELEBRATION	Enjoying self – gifts; talents; abilities;			
	Achievements and victories			
	Progress and potential			

Stage		
symbol		

ME

SELF-AWARENESS

I can...

BODY		I can...								
	Movement	I can move and be still on command.								
		I can move confidently.								
		I can move different parts of my body on command.								
		I can create chaotic movement.								
	Control	I can change the speed of my movement.								
		I can use touch appropriately.								
		I can use space appropriately.								
	Expression	I can change the tone of my movement.								
		I can create atmosphere with my movement.								
		I can communicate emotion with my movement.								
		I can tell a story with my movement.								
		I can connect with others through touch.								

Stage							
symbol							

11

SELF-AWARENESS   I can...

ME

EMOTIONS

	I can...											
Accurately identify feelings	I can identify happy, sad, shocked, angry.	I can identify more subtle emotions.	I can identify overtly fake emotions.	I can accurately identify my emotions.								
Comfortable vs uncomfortable emotions					I can identify emotions that are comfortable for me.	I can identify emotions that are uncomfortable for me.	I can identify feelings and sensations that accom-pany uncomfortable emotions.					
Sharing personal feelings								I can share comfortable emotions and feelings.	I can share uncomfortable feelings.	I can discuss difficult situations after the moment has passed.	I can talk about challenging situations in the mo-ment.	I can share my feelings appropriately with others.

Stage	
symbol	

ME

SELF-AWARENESS

I can...

PERSONALITY	I can...	
Personality types	I can use a simple personality test to identify my personality type.	
	I can identify strengths in my personality.	
	I can identify challenges in having my personality type.	
	I can make a plan for making the most of being me.	
Likes and dis-likes	I can identify things, actions, situations and words I like.	
	I can identify things, actions, situations and words I don't like.	
	I can explain and discuss my likes and dislikes.	
Strengths and goals	I can identify a talent, skill or ability I have.	
	I can identify a character trait I have that it admirable.	
	I can identify something that I can do better.	
	I can make a goal and plan to improve in an area that I feel challenging.	

Stage	
symbol	

13

SELF-AWARENESS

ME

EXPERIENCE

I can...

		I can...
Core memo-ries	I can identify important childhood memories.	
	I can identify how that core memory made me/them feel.	
	I can identify the 'life lesson' I/they got from that core memory.	
	I can identify how the 'life lesson' has affected my life since.	
Influence	I can identify someone or something that influences me.	
	I can explain why and how influence happens.	
	I can identify negative and positive influence.	
Experience re-perceived	I can identify the effects of motivation on situations.	
	I can re-imagine an experience by exploring different influences and 'life lessons'.	
	I can separate myself from a situation and judge from different view points.	
	I can explore my actions and choices 'out of role' as an observer.	

Stage	
symbol	

ME

SELF-AWARENESS — I can...

CELEBRATION	I can...								
Enjoying self – gifts; talents; abilities;	I have identified my gifts/talents/abilities.								
	I have shared my gifts/talents/abilities.								
	I have explored a gift/talent/ability.								
	I have demonstrated a gift/talent/ability.								
achievements and victories	I have identified a victory/success/achievement.								
	I have shared my victory/success/achievement.								
	I have celebrated my victory/success/achievement.								
Potential & progress	I have identified a challenge I face.								
	I have planned and prepared for success.								
	I have practiced my challenge with safe-space drama.								
	I have made the progress from my plan in safe-space drama.								
	I have made the progress from my plan in a real situation.								

Stage				
symbol				

15

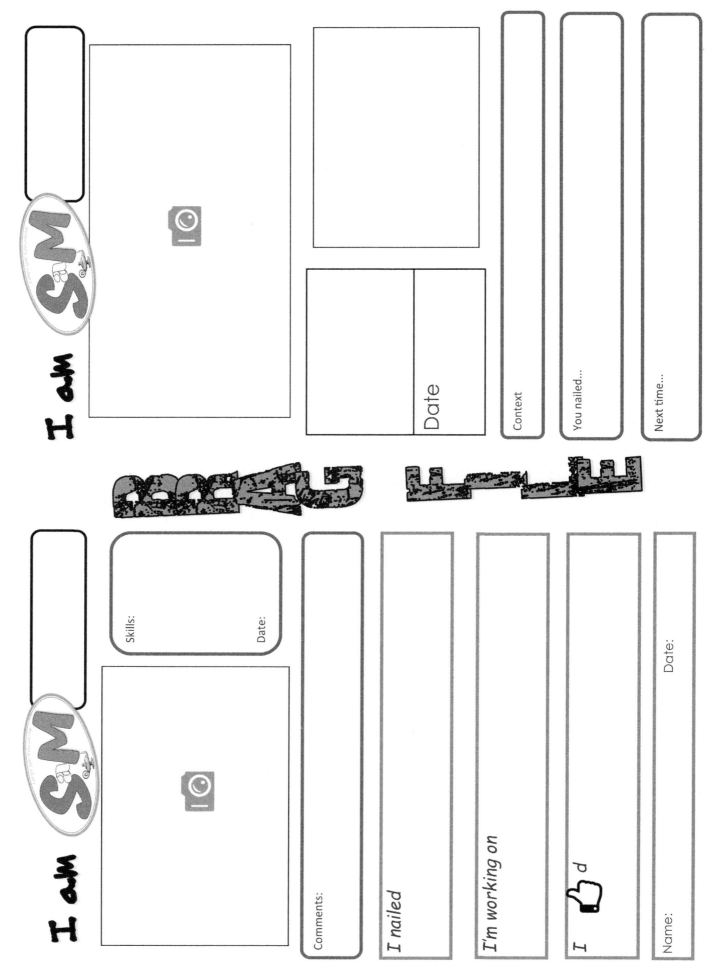

I am

Skills:

Date:

Comments:

I nailed

I'm working on

I d

Name:

Date:

I am

Date

Context

You nailed...

Next time...

16

ME

Self-Awareness

Confidence

Self-Regulation
H.O.P.E.

I am S∂M

CONFIDENCE

ME — skills overview

			Stage	symbol
FINDING MY VOICE	Seeking help	I can ask for help when I need it.		
	Sharing opinions and ideas	I can share my thoughts and opinions with others.		
	Asking questions	I can ask questions when I don't understand or I want to challenge an idea.		
RISK	Self-expression	I can express my self through a variety of ways.		
	Stepping out to try new things	I can try new things and fully engage.		
	Practicing risk appropriately in different contexts	I can risk moving beyond my comfort zone.		
PROBLEM-SOLVING	Plotting—mapping out all aspects of the problem	I can explore a problem and map out the issues.		
	Process—planning how to navigate the blending of sides	I can make a plan to solve a problem.		
	Packaging—setting boundaries and practicing discussion without aggression.	I can discuss and resolve a problem without any form of aggression.		
EMOTIONAL RESILIENCE	Emotional awareness—emotional response and situational geography	I can identify what I am experiencing as temporary and see a future beyond now.		
	Identifying and using prompts, reminders and strategies	I can identify and use positive strategies to manage my emotions in a situation.		
	Identifying triggers and appropriateness	I can identify triggers to difficult emotions and appropriate responses.		
CELEBRATION	Enjoying self – gifts; talents; abilities;			
	Achievements and victories			
	Potential and progress			

18

CONFIDENCE   I can...

ME

FINDING MY VOICE

SEEKING HELP	I can ask for help from peers.	
	I can ask for help from adults.	
	I can identify appropriate help for situations.	
SHARING OPINIONS AND IDEAS	I can share simple/agreeing opinions.	
	I can share conflicting/new opinions and ideas.	
	I can share opinions and ideas that are sensitive to me.	
ASKING QUESTIONS	I can ask questions one to one and in a small group.	
	I can ask questions in a large group.	
	I can ask questions that make me feel vulnerable.	

Stage	
symbol	

19

ME

CONFIDENCE   I can...

RISK		
SELF-EXPRESSION	I can share my thoughts and feelings with others.	
	I can disagree with others.	
	I can communicate my passion to others.	
STEPPING OUT TO TRY NEW THINGS	I can try something outside of my comfort zone.	
	I can speak out in front of others with confidence.	
	I can perform passion, belief and conviction in safe-space drama.	
PRACTICING RISK IN DIFFERENT CONTEXTS	I can practice risk one to one.	
	I can practice risk in safe-space drama.	
	I can practice risk in live contexts.	

Stage						
symbol						

20

CONFIDENCE

I can...

ME

PROBLEM-SOLVING		I can...				
PLOTTING	I can map out my side of a problem.					
	I can map out other sides of a problem.					
	I can map out potential pitfalls of a problem.					
PROCESS	I can plan out the process of problem-solving.					
	I can make a plan for problem-solving.					
	I can navigate the problem using my plan.					
PACKAGING	I can set boundaries for the discussion.					
	I can identify responses to avoid to keep the peace.					
	I can practice discussion without aggression in safe-space drama.					

Stage						
symbol						

ME

CONFIDENCE   I can...

EMOTIONAL RESILIENCE

EMOTIONAL AWARENESS	I can identify how I am feeling and how my emotions are developing, landmarks and destinations				
	I can outline and workshop typical examples of emotional journeys in safe-space drama.				
	I can identify and use stops in my journey where intervention will work best.				
PROMPTS	I can identify landmarks, destinations and plan prompts for me on my emotional response journey.				
	I can use mapping to regulate with prompts.				
	I can use mapping and self-regulate.				
TRIGGERS	I can identify triggers and appropriate responses.				
	I can practice appropriateness in safe-space drama.				
	I can explore and workshop strategies and outcomes in safe-space drama.				

Stage	
symbol	

22

I am

I am SM

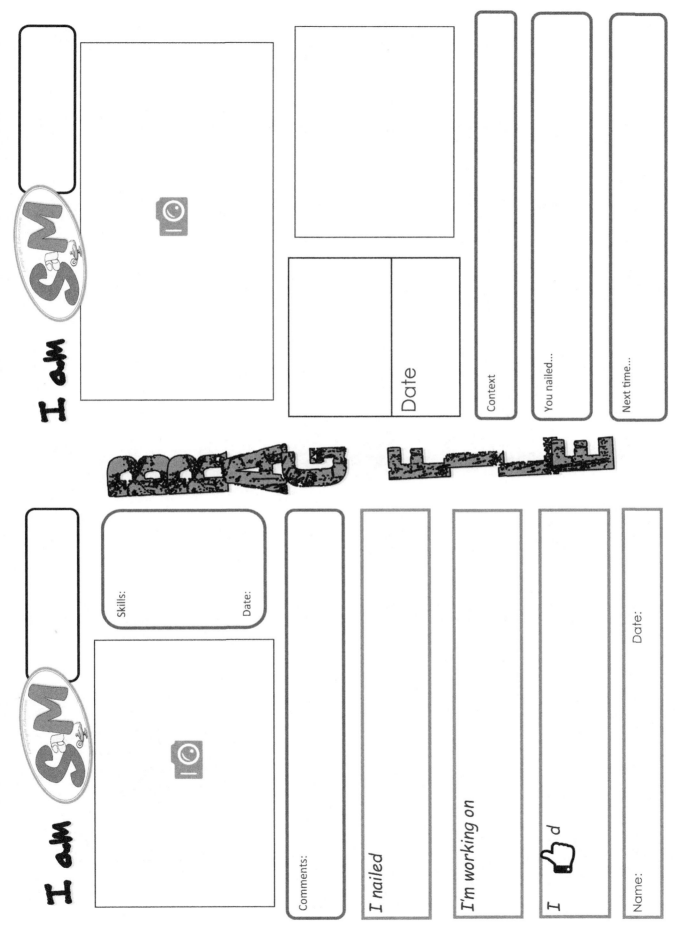

Date

Context

You nailed…

Next time…

Skills:

Date:

Comments:

I nailed

I'm working on

I d

Name: _____ Date:

23

ME

Self-Awareness
Confidence

Self-Regulation

H.O.P.E.

I am

ME

SELF-REGULATION *skills overview*

Category	Descriptor	Statement
STRATEGIES	Explore a variety of strategies and their effects on regulation.	I can explore strategies and their effectiveness for me.
	Toolkit—developing a variety of strategies, plan and prepare.	I can plan and prepare a toolkit of strategies to help myself.
	Trials—using the toolkit	I can practice using my strategies in live trials.
INTERVENTION	Enabled self-regulation safe-space	I can respond to others assisting me in using my strategies.
	Prompted self-regulation safe-space	I can respond to the prompts of others to use my strategies
	Independent self-regulation safe-space	I can self-regulate independently using my strategies.
PROCESSING	Inside - outside: emotional v situational	I can explore the difference between feelings and situation.
	Your side – my side: changing viewpoints	I can explore the difference between my and others' viewpoints.
	Upside – downside: weighing our responses	I can explore the positives and negatives of my responses.
PRACTICE	Dealing with challenging emotions out of time—hindsight	I can discuss challenging emotions I have experienced.
	Dealing with challenging emotions at the time—in the moment	I can discuss challenging emotions I am experiencing.
	Dealing with challenging emotions before time—pre-empting	I can discuss challenging emotions I can predict I will feel.
CELEBRATION	Enjoying self – gifts; talents; abilities;	
	achievements and victories	
	challenges & progress	

Stage		
symbol		

SELF-REGULATION

ME

I can...

STRATEGIES

STRATEGIES	I can...		
EXPLORE A VARIETY OF STRATEGIES AND THEIR EFFECTS ON REGULATION.	I can identify when I feel peaceful.		
	I have explored a variety of strategies and reflected on how they impact me.		
	I have chosen strategies that help me feel peaceful.		
PREPARE AND PLAN A TOOLKIT OF STRATEGIES FOR EFFECTIVE REGULATION.	I have identified triggers to my dysregulation.		
	I have identified effective strategies for different journeys towards being peaceful.		
	I have prepared what I need to use my strategies when I need to.		
PRACTICE USING TOOLKIT IN SAFE SPACE DRAMA, WORKSHOPPING AND LIVE TRIALS.	I can use my strategies for 5 minutes unaided.		
	I have practiced using my toolkit in safe-space workshops.		
	I have used my toolkit in live trials and reflected on their effectiveness.		

Stage	
symbol	

26

SELF-REGULATION

I can...

ME

INTERVENTION

	I can...
ENABLED	I can use my strategies when instructed.
	I can use the strategy I am guided towards from my toolkit.
	I can use my strategy for 5 minutes under supervision.
PROMPTED	I can use my strategies when prompted.
	I can choose my strategy when prompted.
	I can use my strategy continuously for 5 minutes with prompts.
INDEPENDENT	I can identify the best time to use my strategy.
	I can identify the type of dysregulation I am experiencing and choose the best strategy to use.
	I can use my strategies to regulate at the most effective time and for the chosen length of time.

Stage	
symbol	

SELF-REGULATION

ME

I can...

PROCESSING	I can...				
INSIDE & OUTISDE	I can explain a basic situation in safe-space drama.				
	I can explore a character's emotions about that situation.				
	I can identify how the inside emotions and the outside situations affect each other.				
YOUR SIDE & MY SIDE	I can explain a situation from one character's point of view.				
	I can explain the same situation from another point of view.				
	I can explore real life situations from my point of view and the points of view of others.				
UPSIDE & DOWNSIDE	I can identify the positive and negative effects of a #character's response to a situation.				
	I can identify positives in real life responses to situations.				
	I can identify positives that could be found by changing responses to situations.				

Stage	
symbol	

28

ME

SELF-REGULATION   I can...

PRACTICE		
OUT OF TIME	I can explore difficult situations in safe-space drama.	
	I can explore character emotions in safe space drama.	
	I can workshop real life situations through safe-space drama and explore alternative responses.	
AT THE TIME	I can use key image, marking the moment, hot-seating and other techniques to explore current situations.	
	I can workshop alternative responses to ongoing situations and collaborate in forum theatre to explore the responses of others.	
BEFORE TIME	I can devise drama from realistic and familiar situations and explore emotional journeys.	
	I can use drama techniques to identify responses most likely to bring a good outcome for all.	
	I can devise drama to demonstrate the learning of how to respond to challenges in a healthy way.	

Stage	
symbol	

29

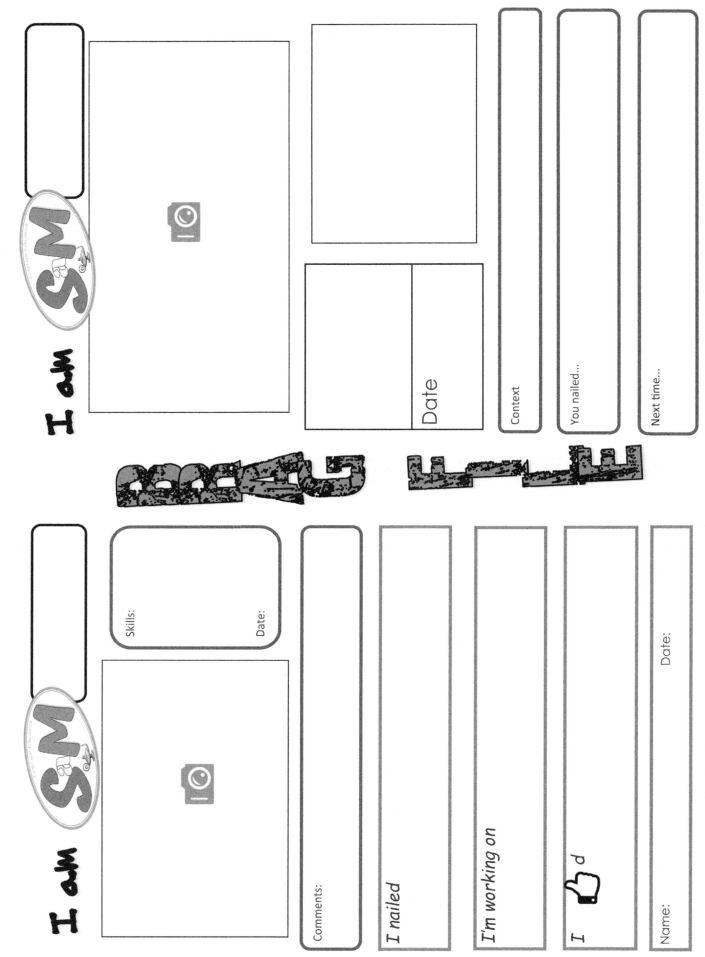

I am SM

Date

Context

You nailed...

Next time...

I am SM

Skills:

Date:

Comments:

I nailed

I'm working on

I

Name:

Date:

30

ME

Self-Awareness
Confidence
Self-Regulation

H.O.P.E.

**Honouring the Optomistic Potential
and Engaging**

I am

ME

H.O.P.E.

Honouring the Optimistic Potential & Engaging

skills overview

Category	Skill	Description
CHANGE	Prepare	I can identify changes and prepare for them.
	Navigate and settle	I can navigate change and settle myself.
	Reward and reflect	I can identify victories and reflect on responses.
TIME PERSPECTIVE	Past	I can identify a past moment with different emotions.
	Future	I can identify future promise and potential.
	Present with perspective	I can adjust and balance my responses to the present challenges.
VICTORY INVENTORY	Past conquering	I can identify past achievements and victories.
	Peer conquering	I can identify victories in others.
	Potential conquering	I can identify opportunities and paths to victory.
REFLECT	Praise – self-encouragement	I can use real praise to encourage myself.
	Past-problems -changing land-scape	I can explore the journey through past problems.
	Seeing success in perceived failure	I can identify good things coming from situations where it may appear I have failed.
CELEBRATION	Enjoying self – gifts; talents; abilities;	I can demonstrate enjoyment of my giftings.
	achievements and victories	I can celebrate my victories and achievements.
	challenges & progress	I can identify challenges and plot my progress.

Stage	
symbol	

strengths

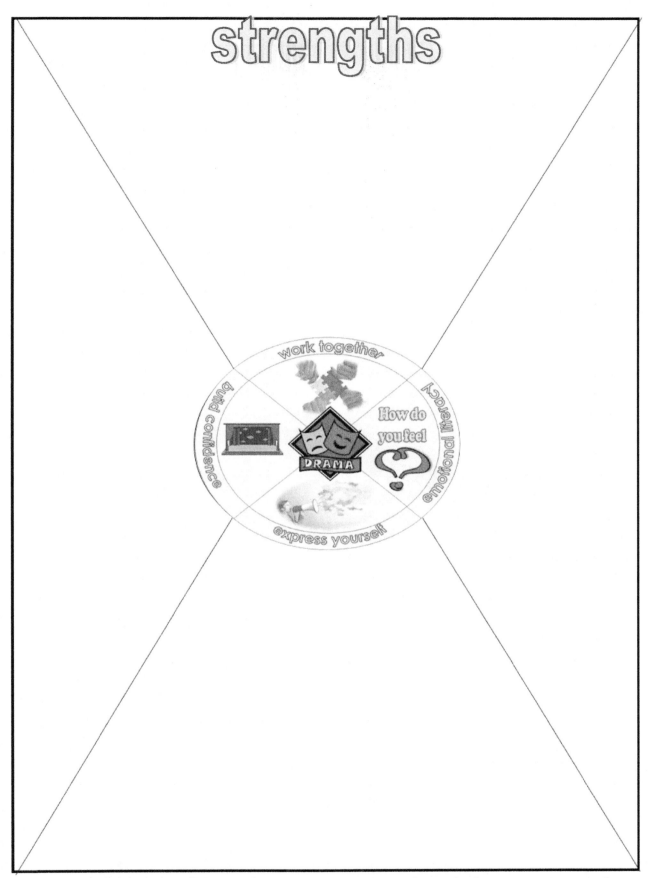

Put your reward stickers in the correct category and watch them grow to see where your strengths lie and where you can challenge yourself more.

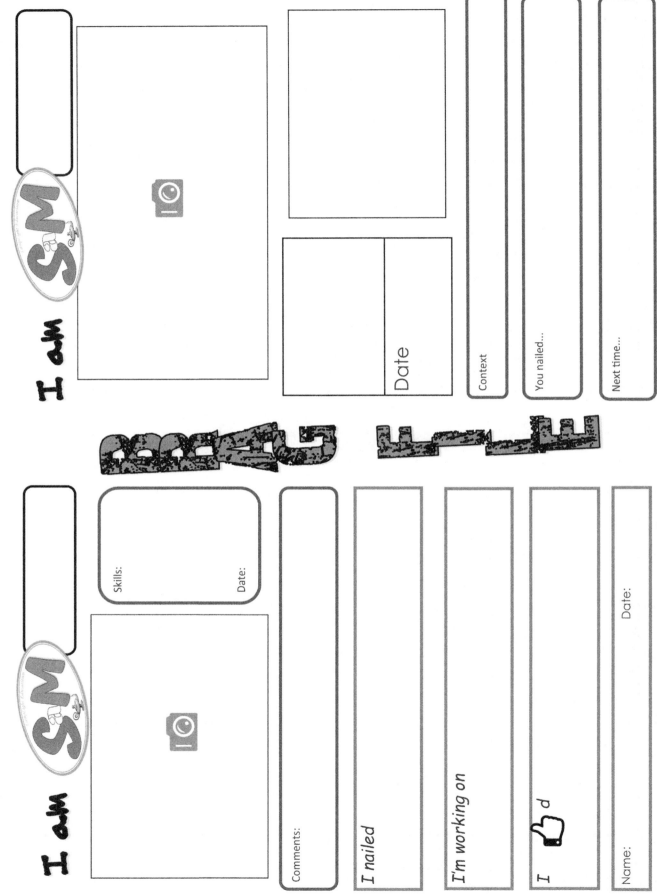

I am

Date

Context

You nailed...

Next time...

Skills:

Date:

Comments:

I nailed

I'm working on

I 👆 d

Name:

Date:

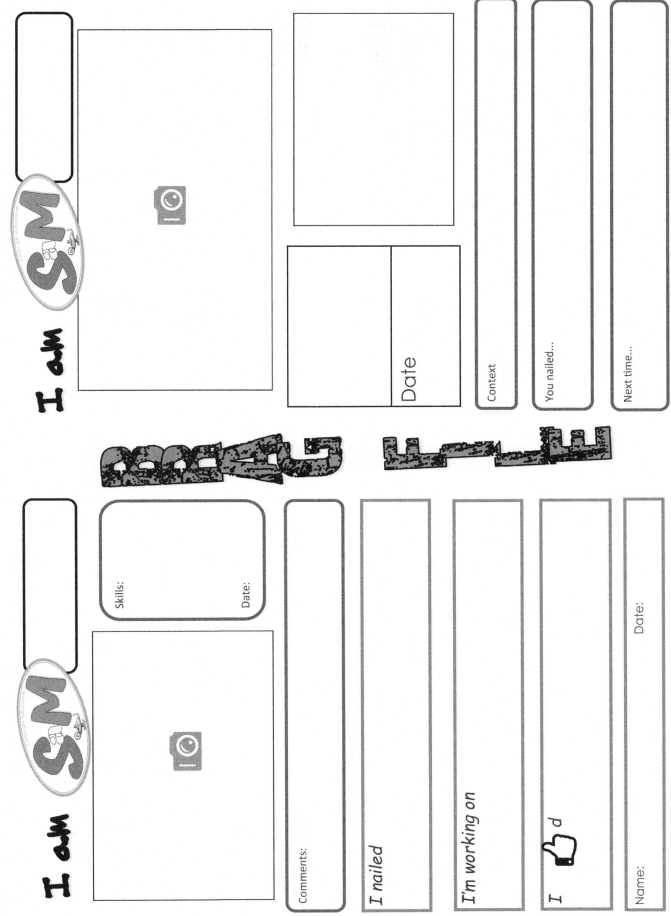

I am

SAM

Date

Context

You nailed...

Next time...

I am

SAM

Skills:

Date:

Comments:

I nailed

I'm working on

I 👆 d

Name:

Date:

35

WE

Empathy
Connection
Problem-Solving
Healthy Leadership

I am

WE EMPATHY
skills overview

			Stage	
READING OTHERS	Body language; vocal & facial expression	I can understand what others are communicating through their bodies, voices and faces.		
	Words	I can understand simple meanings in word choices		
	Actions	I can understand simple meanings in actions.		
READING SITUATIONS	Emotions as responses	I can explore emotions as responses to events.		
	Emotions in contexts	I can explore emotions in different contexts.		
	Identifying roles and goals	I can identify roles and goals in situations.		
SYMPATHY	Understanding the feelings of others	I can identify, explain and predict others' emotions.		
	Connecting with others' feelings	I can connect feelings I have experienced to the feelings being experienced by others.		
	Exercising patience and kindness	I can exercise patience and kindness in others' distress.		
IDENTIFICATION	Relating to others' experience	I can relate personal experience to those of others.		
	Relating to others' situations	I can relate personal situations to those of others.		
	Responding sensitively	I can respond to others with appropriate kindness.		
REFLECTION	Strengths and challenges	I can identify my own strengths and challenges.		
	Separating from us and others	I can separate myself from situations to reflect.		
	Clean slate approach	I can give myself and others a fresh start after reflection on a challenging situation.		

Stage	
symbol	

EMPATHY

WE

BODY LANGUAGE, VOCAL AND FACIAL EXPRESSION	I can read meanings in others' body language.	
	I can read meanings in others' vocal expression.	
	I can read meanings in others' facial expression.	
WORDS	I can understand meanings of others' word choices.	
	I can interpret the word choices of playwrights to communicate meaning.	
	I can choose words to communicate meaning of my own.	
ACTIONS	I can interpret the stage directions in a script and meanings being communicated.	
	I can explore the meanings of others' use of movement.	
	I can use movement to express my understanding of the feelings, connections and emotions of others.	

READING OTHERS

Stage	
symbol	

EMPATHY

WE

READING SITUATIONS

EMOTIONS AS RESPONSES	I can identify expected emotional responses to events.
	I can predict different characters' emotional responses to stimuli.
	I can explore the emotional responses of others in safe-space drama workshops.
EMOTIONS IN CONTEXTS	I can identify expected emotional responses to situations.
	I can predict understandable responses to contexts in safe-space drama.
	I can explore the effects of different emotional responses to situations.
IDENTIFYING ROLES AND GOALS	I can identify roles of characters in situations.
	I can identify motivations for different characters in situations.
	I can explore the benefits of different responses to others through the use of goal/role adjustment.

Stage	
symbol	

39

EMPATHY

WE

SYMPATHY

IDENTIFYING AND UNDERSTANDING OTHERS' FEELINGS	I can identify emotions communicated by others.	
	I can explore the feelings and responses of characters in drama workshop.	
	I can explore the feelings and responses of others in safe-space drama.	
CONNECTING WITH OTHERS' FEELINGS	I can connect situations to personal experience.	
	I can connect the emotional states and landscapes of others to personal experience.	
	I can express the feelings of others in safe-space drama.	
PATIENCE AND KINDNESS UNDER FIRE	I can identify dysregulation and stress in others.	
	I can explore challenges from and responses to the dysregulation of others.	
	I can exercise patience and kindness in responding to the dysregulation of others.	

Stage	
symbol	

EMPATHY

IDENTIFICATION	**RELATING TO OTHERS' EXPERIENCES**	I can compare the experiences of others.
		I can explore the similarities and differences in situations.
		I can use safe-space drama to create situations that are similar to other experiences.
	RELATING TO OTHERS' SITUATIONS	I can identify the needs of characters in situations.
		I can explore personal responses of others in drama workshops.
		I can express the needs of others in safe-space drama.
	RESPONDING SENSITIVELY	I can identify helpful responses to others.
		I can explore different responses to others.
		I can respond sensitively to others.

Stage	
symbol	

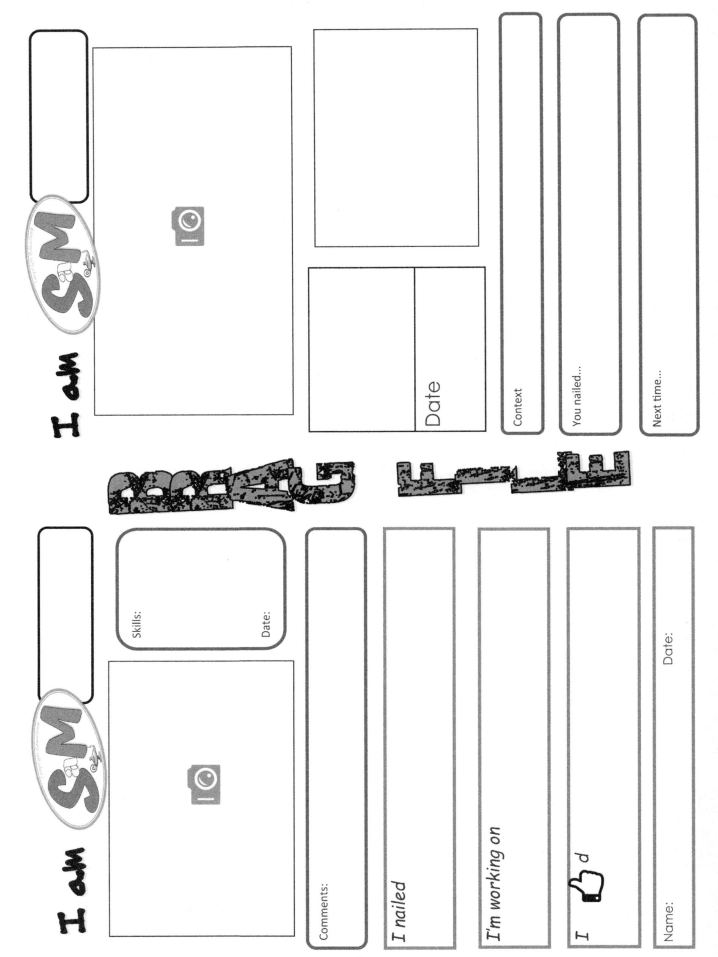

I am

Date

Context

You nailed...

Next time...

I am

Skills:

Date:

Comments:

I nailed

I'm working on

I d

Name:

Date:

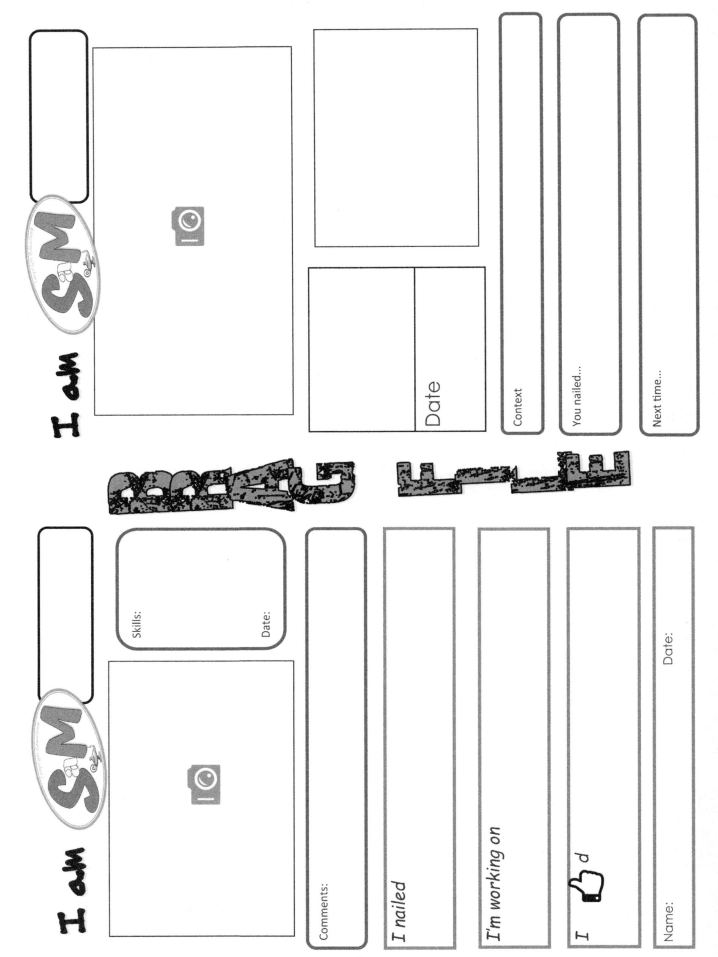 (contd.)

42

WE

Empathy

Connection

Problem-Solving

Healthy Leadership

I am

43

WE CONNECTION

skills overview

Category	Subtopic	Skill statement
COMMUNICATION	Honesty with kindness	I can tell the truth kindly.
	Engagement and maintaining healthy interactions	I can maintain healthy communication with others.
	Appropriateness	I can communicate appropriately to others.
LISTENING	Cues	I can use listening cues to promote connection.
	Strategies	I can use simple strategies to listen well to others.
	Exercising patience	I can exercise patience in listening to others,
LANGUAGES	Personality types	I can identify different personality types.
	Modes of expression	I can identify different methods of expression.
	Speaking their way	I can communicate in a way that values the other person.
RISK	Initiating connection	I can begin a drama sequence.
	Expectation and control	I can identify expectations of connection and types of control.
	New actions/words/voices/roles; new Me; new We.	I can become a character very different from myself.
BOUNDARIES	Physical; contact	I can identify and set physical boundaries for myself and others.
	Emotional & psychological	I can explore and express emotional and psychological boundaries.
	Contextual appropriateness	I can explore how boundaries change with context.

Stage			
symbol			

WE CONNECTION

COMMUNICATION

	I can...					
HONESTY WITH KINDNESS	I can identify rudeness.					
	I can identify my truth.					
	I can speak my truth using kind word choices and expressions.					
ENGAGEMENT AND MAINTAINING HEALTHY INTERACTIONS	I can listen actively.					
	I can listen and respond to others kindly.					
	I can negotiate and compromise to create harmony.					
APPROPRIATENESS	I can make appropriate word choices.					
	I can identify disrespectful expressions.					
	I can select appropriate time, place and manner to communicate to others.					

Stage						
symbol						

WE CONNECTION

I can...

LISTENING

CUES	I can identify sound cues of listening.	
	I can identify physical cues of listening.	
	I can use a variety of cues to show someone I am listening.	
STRATEGIES	I can identify strategies for active listening.	
	I can plan the use of strategies for active listening.	
	I can use active listening strategies.	
EXERCISING PATIENCE	I can listen without interrupting the speaker.	
	I can listen without expressing anger.	
	I can listen and collaborate with other points of view rather than just argue.	

Stage	
symbol	

WE

CONNECTION

LANGUAGES		I can...							
PERSONALITY TYPES	I can respond to questions about my personality.								
	I can identify my personality type and recognise myself in it.								
	I can explore how personality types differ.								
MODE OF COMMUNICATION	I can identify my ways of communicating.								
	I can identify others' communication types..								
	I can explore how knowing communication types can help in relationships.								
SPEAKING THEIR WAY	I can identify opportunities for speaking someone else's language.								
	I can explore changes in communication with someone I know.								
	I can explore how situations can change by changing my communication choices.								

Stage							
symbol							

WE CONNECTION

I can...

RISK	**INITIATING CONNECTION**	I can begin a conversation with someone.				
		I can begin a conversation about emotions with someone.				
		I can respond to someone else's conversation by asking about their emotions.				
	EXPECTATION AND CONTROL	I can identify social expectations of roles and responsibilities.				
		I can identify the negative and positive expectations others may have of me.				
		I can identify my own expectations of others and make allowances.				
	EXPERIMENT IN PERFORMANCE AND EXPRESSION	I can become a character very different from myself.				
		I can express myself in different ways and forms.				
		I can explore how changes in expression and expectation can change responses.				

Stage	
symbol	

WE CONNECTION

I can...

BOUNDARIES						
PHYSICAL: CONTACT AND SPACE	I can identify my personal space and that of others.					
	I can use proxemics to communicate appropriately in performance.					
	I can use contact and proxemics to tell a story.					
EMOTIONAL AND PSYCHOLOGICAL	I can identify healthy boundaries.					
	I can explore characters without boundaries.					
	I can maintain healthy boundaries.					
CONTEXTUAL APPROPRIATENESS	I can read people and situations and identify appropriate behaviours and expectations.					
	I can explore appropriate behaviours in safe-space workshopping.					
	I can maintain appropriate relationships within the Drama space.					

Stage						
symbol						

49

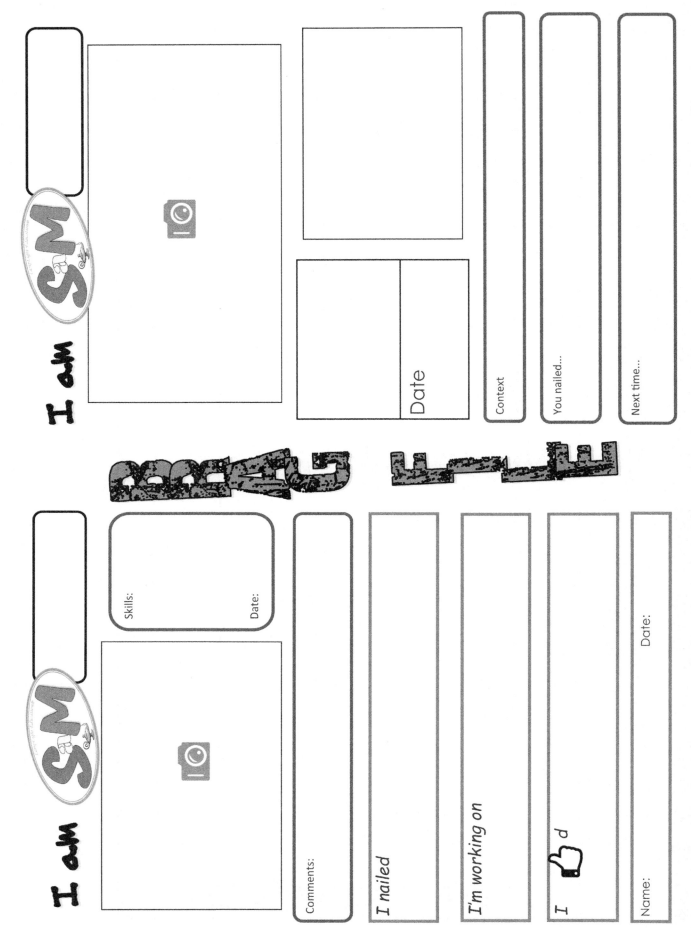

I am SM

Date

Context

You nailed…

Next time…

I am SM

Skills:

Date:

Comments:

I nailed

I'm working on

I 👍 d

Name:

Date:

WE

Empathy

Connection

Problem-Solving

Healthy Leadership

I am

WE PROBLEM-SOLVING
skills overview

SAMENESS & DIFFERENCE	Common ground	I can identify things I have in common with others.
	Perceptions of others	I can explore the judgements I make about characters.
	New ground	I can identify differences that can strengthen others.
VALUE	Strengths and limitations	I can identify strengths and limitations in a character.
	Positive words	I can use positive words to describe characters.
	Roles and goals	I can explore goals and roles within a piece of drama.
	Peace or friction?	I can identify responses that bring 'peace' or 'friction'.
COLLABORA-TION & COM-PROMISE	Group strength and identity	I can explore group identity and strengths to encourage.
	'In other words…'	I can communicate a difficult message positively by word choices.
STRATEGIES	Goal setting; skills inventory and re-sponsibilities	I can set goals, identify skills and assign responsibility within a group.
	Safe-space problem-solving	I can explore methods of problem-solving between characters in safe-space drama.
	Practicing the middle ground	I can find the middle ground in conflict.
CELEBRATION	Strengths and challenges	I can identify strengths and challenges within the group.
	Separating from us and others	I can discuss the effectiveness of the group without becoming per-sonal.
	Clean slate approach	I can give myself and others a fresh start after reflective learning.

Stage	
symbol	

52

WE PROBLEM-SOLVING

I can...

SAMENESS & DIFFERENCE

COMMON GROUND
- I can identify universal sameness and difference.
- I can explore and express aspects of sameness.
- I can explore and express aspects of difference.

PERCEPTIONS OF OTHERS
- I can identify and explore stereotypes.
- I can identify and explore bias and prejudice.
- I can explore different experiences and perspectives in safe-space drama.

NEW GROUND
- I can express difference in character.
- I can create drama demonstrating difference and sameness.
- I can create drama communicating sameness and difference in harmony.

Stage	
symbol	

WE PROBLEM-SOLVING

I can...

VALUE

STRENGTHS AND LIMITATIONS	I can identify strength and limitation in safe-space drama.
	I can explore the benefits of strength expressed in a healthy way.
	I can explore the benefits of limitations expressed in a healthy way.
POSITIVE WORDS	I can identify positive, constructive word choices.
	I can explore the effects of changing word choices on problem-solving.
	I can practice positive word choices in safe-space drama.
ROLES AND GOALS	I can identify different roles in a given situation.
	I can identify different goals in a given situation.
	I can explore the experiences of different roles with different goals in drama workshop.

Stage					
symbol					

WE

PROBLEM-SOLVING

I can...

COLLABORATION & COMPROMISE

Category	I can statements	
PEACE OR FRICTION	I can identify communication that promotes friction.	
	I can identify communication that promotes peace.	
	I can explore different communications and their effects on problem-solving.	
GROUP STRENGTH AND IDENTITY	I can identify group strengths and collective identity.	
	I can apply knowledge of strengths and identify to problem-solving.	
	I can practice promoting group identity and strengths in collaborative work.	
IN OTHER WORDS	I can use deliberate changes in word choices to create a healthy, collaborative group dynamic.	
	I can practice healthy, encouraging communication in collaboration with another person.	
	I can practice healthy, encouraging communication in collaboration with a group of 3 or more people.	

Stage	
symbol	

WE PROBLEM-SOLVING

I can...

STRATEGIES	I can...		
GOAL SETTING, SKILLS INVENTORY AND RESPONSIBILITIES	I can set goals for a group that are worthwhile, challenging and realistic		
	I can accurately identify skills within a small group of 3 or more people.		
	I can allocate responsibilities based upon the goals and the skills of the group.		
SAFE-SPACE PROBLEM-SOLVING— 'SOMEONE ELSE'S SHOES'	I can identify different perspectives from my own.		
	I can explore different perspectives within a small group collaboration.		
	I can identify with others and express their different perspectives as if they were my own.		
PRACTICING THE MIDDLE GROUND	I can identify opposing ideas and perspectives.		
	I can identify aspects of sameness and difference in the different perspectives and ideas.		
	I can identify and persuasively express the virtues of collaborating by exploring the middle ground.		

Stage	
symbol	

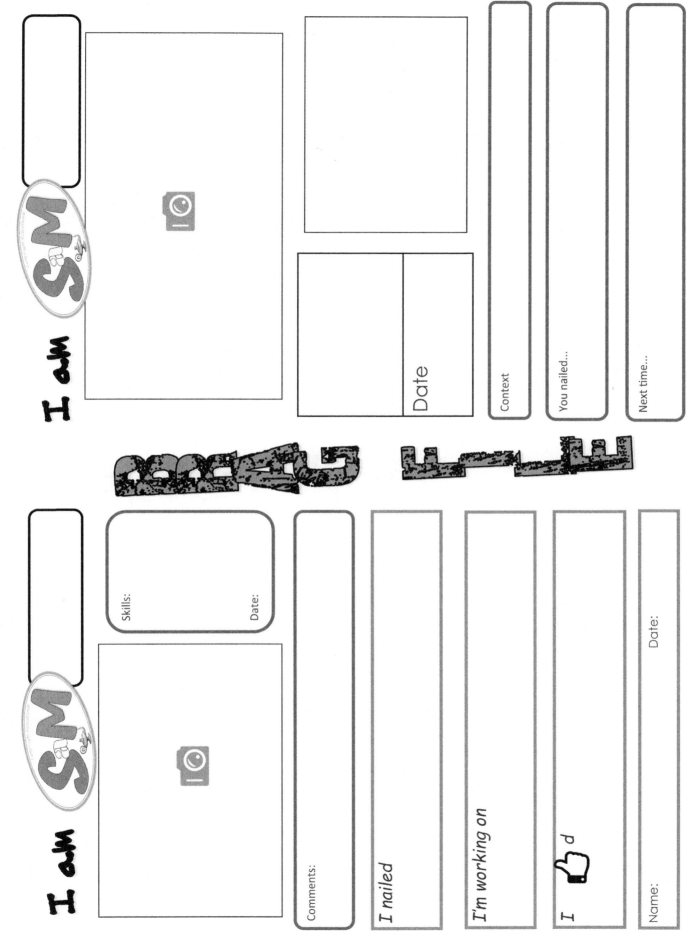

I am

SM

Date

Context

You nailed...

Next time...

Skills:

Date:

Comments:

I nailed

I'm working on

I d

Name:

WE

Empathy
Connection
Problem-Solving

Healthy Leadership

I am

WE HEALTHY-LEADERSHIP

skills overview
I can...

Category	Subcategory	I can...
RELATIONSHIPS	TYPES	I can explore different types of connection.
	TRAITS	I can identify healthy and unhealthy ways of being.
	MAINTENANCE	I can mend and maintain connection.
HUMILITY, PREMISSION AND RESPECT	ACCEPTANCE	I can accept difference and my need for others.
	GRATITUDE	I can express gratitude to others.
	SUPPORT	I can accept help and express desire to appropriately support others.
VALUING VOICE AND RISK	UNIVERSAL VALUE	I can express understanding of the value of others and their differences.
	REWARDING RISK	I can encourage the progress-making risk-taking of others.
	EMPOWERING DIFFERENCE	I can encourage the valuing of difference.
ENCOURAGEMENT AND POWER-SHARING	IDENTIFYING STRENGTHS	I can identify real strengths in others and in situations.
	JOURNEY MINDSET	I can demonstrate the value of the journey over the destination and personalities.
	ENABLING OTHERS	I can encourage and enable responsibility and leadership in others.
CELEBRATION	ENABLING CELEBRATION	I can create opportunities for celebration.
	ACCEPTING OUTCOMES	I can model appropriate acceptance.
	ENCOURAGING OTHERS	I can model appreciation and encouragement of others.

Stage	
symbol	

WE   HEALTHY·LEADERSHIP

I can...

RELATIONSHIPS		I can...			
TYPES	I can identify autocratic leadership.				
	I can identify democratic leadership.				
	I can identify free rein leadership.				
TRAITS	I can identify healthy leadership in contexts.				
	I can explore different leadership styles in different situations.				
	I can identify my own leadership style and choose helpful changes.				
MAINTENANCE	I can choose a leadership style for a given situation.				
	I can reflect on the leadership traits used by others and myself.				
	I can make recommendations for improving my own and others' leadership effectiveness.				

Stage	
symbol	

60

WE   HEALTHY-LEADERSHIP

I can...

HUMILITY, PERMISSION AND RESPECT	I can...							
ACCEPTANCE	I can receive help and advice from others, gratefully.							
	I can offer help and advice to others kindly.							
	I can show respect to others while leading and following.							
GRATITUDE	I can express gratitude to others.							
	I can identify things to be grateful for in any given situation.							
	I can receive and express gratitude in other roles.							
SUPPORT	I can offer support sensitively to others.							
	I can support others appropriately to complete a task.							
	I can support others appropriately in reflection on the task.							

Stage							
symbol							

61

WE

HEALTHY-LEADERSHIP

I can...

VALUING VOICE AND RISK		I can...	
UNIVERSAL VALUE	I can acknowledge the universal value of life.		
	I can express the universal value of others in my choices and leadership.		
	I can explore ways of communicating the universal value of life.		
REWARDING RISK	I can express admiration for the risk taking and voices of others.		
	I can incentivise the self-expression and experimentation of others.		
	I can model self-expression and experimentation in safe-space drama and workshop.		
EMPOWERING DIFFERENCE	I can validate differences in opinions and perspectives.		
	I can explore the differences in experience and values through role-play.		
	I can create opportunities in drama for otherness and difference to be expressed powerfully.		

Stage	
symbol	

WE

HEALTHY·LEADERSHIP

I can...

ENCOURAGEMENT & POWER-SHARING							
IDENTIFYING STRENGTHS	I can delegate responsibilities to others.						
	I can defer authority and place in a task to others.						
	I can make opportunities for others to lead effectively.						
JOURNEY MINDSET	I can demonstrate reflection that prioritises the journey over the end goal.						
	I can explore the benefits of journey-mindset over goal fixation.						
	I can create opportunities for meaningful journeys.						
ENABLING OTHERS	I can listen to others and encourage genuine constructive reflection.						
	I can create opportunities for skill-building in others.						
	I can encourage others to develop their own self-developing opportunities.						

Stage	
symbol	

WE HEALTHY-LEADERSHIP

I can...

CELEBRATION		I can...
ENABLING CELEBRATION	I can create an atmosphere of genuine and meaningful celebration.	
	I can encourage others to celebrate their own and others' successes.	
	I can model creating opportunities for celebration and delegate to others.	
ACCEPTING OUTCOMES	I can model healthy reflection on outcomes.	
	I can demonstrate balanced evaluation of my own and others' work.	
	I can model and encourage in others acceptance and encouraging reflections that inspire positive perseverance.	
ATMOSPHERE OF ENCOURAGEMENT	I can model encouragement.	
	I can create opportunities for encouragement.	
	I can encourage others to develop their own methods of healthy, meaningful encouragement.	

Stage	
symbol	

I am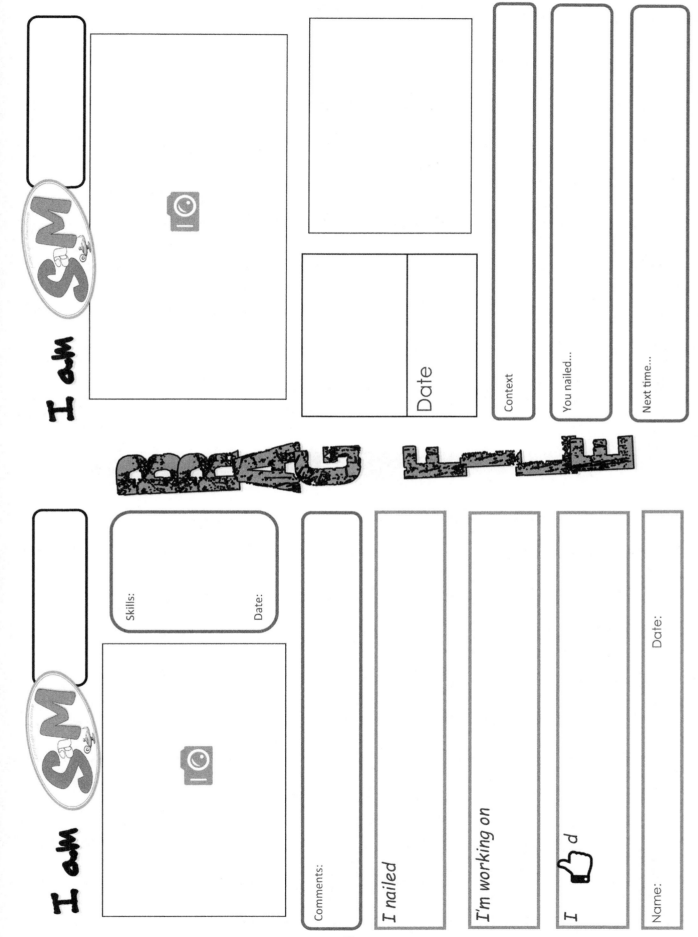

I am

Skills:

Date:

Date

Context

You nailed...

Next time...

Comments:

I nailed

I'm working on

I

d

Name:

Date:

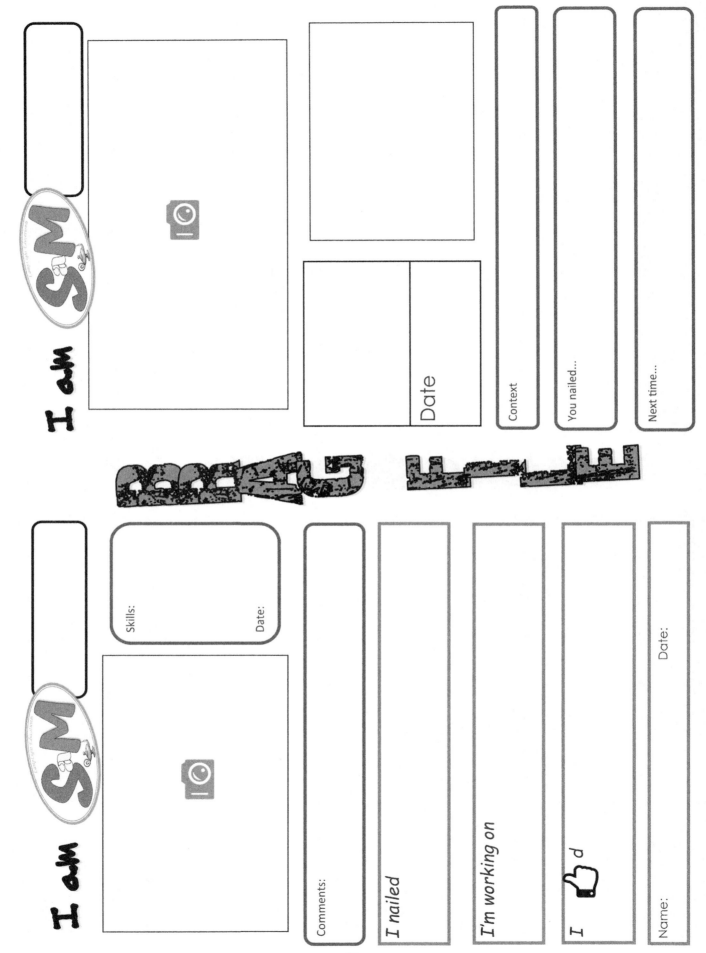

I am

I am

Skills:

Date:

Date

Context

You nailed...

Next time...

Comments:

I nailed

I'm working on

I d

Name:

Date:

SM

I am

My EHCP targets

		succeeding	attempting	experiencing
Long Term Target 1	Step 1			
	Step 2			
	Step 3			
Long Term Target 2	Step 1			
	Step 2			
	Step 3			
Long Term Target 3	Step 1			
	Step 2			
	Step 3			

I am

succeeding

attempting

experiencing

My EHCP targets

Long Term Target 1	Step 1		
	Step 2		
	Step 3		
Long Term Target 2	Step 1		
	Step 2		
	Step 3		
Long Term Target 3	Step 1		
	Step 2		
	Step 3		

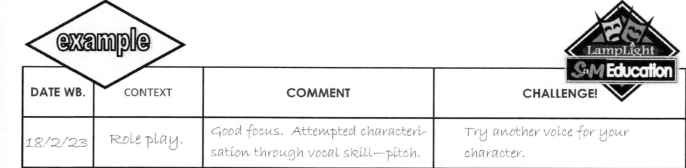

DATE WB.	CONTEXT	COMMENT	CHALLENGE!
18/2/23	Role play.	Good focus. Attempted characterisation through vocal skill—pitch.	Try another voice for your character.

DATE WB.	CONTEXT	COMMENT	CHALLENGE!

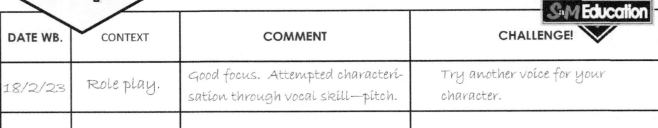

DATE WB.	CONTEXT	COMMENT	CHALLENGE!
18/2/23	Role play.	Good focus. Attempted characterisation through vocal skill—pitch.	Try another voice for your character.

DATE WB.	CONTEXT	COMMENT	CHALLENGE!

Trigger Tracker Pro

Stages	What happened...	But, I could have...
back-ground		
situation		
feeling		
action		
consequence		

Trigger Tracker Pro

Stages	What happened...	But, I could have...
back-ground	The first time something like this happened in my life...	
situation		
feeling		
action		
consequence		

Good things about me:

ways of being

character

personality

My successes:

challenges conquered

victories

fears confronted

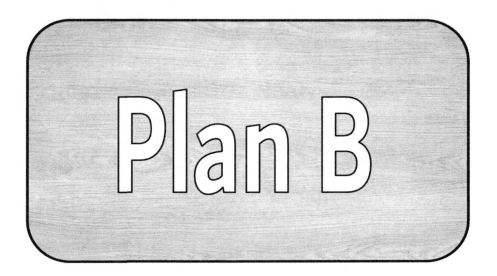

Materials for sessions where the usual leader is absent.

Plan B!

This section contains creative activities for students to do... if lesson cover is required.

Space for your own original mosaic art!

Things to do...

Create a short drama using costume, starting with the line:

How can I help?

Remember to keep it going with friction, but control the flames! (No yelling, touching or throwing)

Think about your favourite character from TV, film or stage and

Hot-seat!

Someone take the chair and, as if you actually were that character, answer questions from the rest of the group. Don't forget to swap and take turns.

Who are you going to call?!

Using the telephone prop, take turns making different kinds of calls:

*   *Takeaway order*

*   *Emergency 999*

*   *To a friend*

Don't forget to use vocal expression—making the emotion fit the context.

Extension: someone use the other phone to answer the call!

Take a problem and work it out like it should be:

Create a drama in a group, telling the story. Try using physical theatre, ensemble or mime.

Things to do... continued

Create a short drama using costume, starting with the lines:

A: Why did you do it?

B: I didn't.

Remember to keep it going with friction, but control the flames! (No yelling, touching or throwing)

Choose a choice that someone might have to make and all the thoughts they might have about it —for and against. Then arrange yourselves into two lines, to make a tunnel of people, and whisper all the thoughts to a person who walks down the middle. Let everyone have a go walking down the middle

Thought Tunnel!

Reflect on what it felt like to walk down the tunnel among all the whis-

pers and consider what decision you would make.

Who are you going to call?! *Using the telephone props:*

* *One person call for help*
* *One person answer and try to help.*

   Don't forget to use vocal expression—making the emotion fit the context.

Take turns asking and answering. What does good asking and answering look like?

PUPPET-SHOW!

Using the puppets: give them voices different to your own

and create a drama that shows the characters resolving a

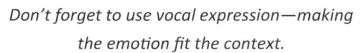

problem.

Thank you for taking your journey with the
Succeeding As Me - Curriculum

Visit our website for resources to support you as you
work towards making the very most of being you.

www.lamplightdrama.com

Printed in Great Britain
by Amazon

45084784R00046